POINTS OF VIEW

Should the
DRIVING AGE
Be Raised?

By Layla Owens

Published in 2023 by
KidHaven Publishing, an Imprint of Greenhaven Publishing, LLC
29 E. 21st Street
New York, NY 10010

Copyright © 2023 KidHaven Publishing, an Imprint of Greenhaven Publishing, LLC.

All rights reserved. No part of this book may be reproduced in any form without permission in writing from the publisher, except by a reviewer.

Designer: Deanna Paternostro
Editor: Caitie McAneney

Photo credits: Cover Anna Hoychuk/Shutterstock.com; p. 5 Motortion Films/Shutterstock.com; p. 7 digitalskillet/Shutterstock.com; pp. 9, 21 (inset, middle) Monkey Business Images/Shutterstock.com; p. 11 Monika Wisniewska/Shutterstock.com; p. 13 tommaso79/Shutterstock.com; pp. 15, 21 (inset, left) Lopolo/Shutterstock.com; p. 17 Nejron Photo/Shutterstock.com; p. 19 SpeedKingz/ Shutterstock.com; p. 21 (notepad) ESB Professional/Shutterstock.com; p. 21 (markers) Kucher Serhii/ Shutterstock.com; p. 21 (photo frame) FARBAI/iStock/Thinkstock; p. 21 (inset, right) Sergey Furtaev/ Shutterstock.com.

Cataloging-in-Publication Data

Names: Owens, Layla.
Title: Should the driving age be raised? / Layla Owens.
Description: New York : KidHaven Publishing, 2023. | Series: Points of view | Includes glossary and index.
Identifiers: ISBN 9781534541979 (pbk.) | ISBN 9781534541993 (library bound) | ISBN 9781534541986 (6pack) | ISBN 9781534542006 (ebook)
Subjects: LCSH: Teenage automobile drivers–United States–Juvenile literature. | Drivers' licenses–United States–Juvenile literature.
Classification: LCC HE5620.J8 O94 2023 | DDC 629.28'30835–dc23

Printed in the United States of America

Some of the images in this book illustrate individuals who are models. The depictions do not imply actual situations or events.

CPSIA compliance information: Batch #CSKH23: For further information contact Greenhaven Publishing LLC, New York, New York at 1-844-317-7404.

Please visit our website, www.greenhavenpublishing.com. For a free color catalog of all our high-quality books, call toll free 1-844-317-7404 or fax 1-844-317-7405.

Find us on

CONTENTS

In the Driver's Seat	4
Laws Around the World	6
Safety First	8
Tougher Tests	10
Maturity Matters	12
Learning by Doing	14
Get a Move On!	16
Busy Lives	18
Who Should Drive?	20
Glossary	22
For More Information	23
Index	24

In the Driver's
SEAT

In some parts of the United States, a person can earn their driver's **license** at 16 years old. This is the minimum driving age. They can also get a learner's **permit** by the time they're between 14 and 16 years old, depending on the state. With a learner's permit, a person can learn to drive a car under the **supervision** of a licensed adult driver.

Some people think that teens aren't **mature** enough for driving. Other people agree with the **minimum** age because it gives teens more freedom. Let's look at both sides of the issue!

Know the Facts!

In some U.S. states, you must be at least 18 years old to have a full driver's license, which means one with no special rules.

It's important to know your state's laws about the minimum driving age. Each state is a little different.

Laws Around the
WORLD

Different countries and states have different minimum ages for driving. Many require a person to take a written test to earn a permit. Then, if they pass a driving test, they can have a restricted license, or a license with special rules. A full license allows people to drive anywhere for any reason.

In El Salvador, a person can get a full driver's license at just 15 years old. In Canada and Australia, a person can get a full driver's license at 16 years old. In most of Europe, Asia, and Africa, you must be 18 years old to have a full driver's license.

Know the Facts!

About 78 percent of countries in the world set the minimum age for a full driver's license at 18.

A restricted license allows drivers to drive for specific reasons, such as going to work. You can't just drive around with friends for fun.

Safety FIRST

Some people want the minimum driving age to be raised because of safety. They don't think 16-year-olds are ready for this kind of responsibility—something they're in charge of.

They point to statistics, or numbers, that show teen drivers are at greater **risk** of car crashes. The Centers for Disease Control and Prevention (CDC) say that teens are at a higher crash risk for the first few months after getting a license. The rate of car crashes per mile is about 1.5 times higher for 16-year-olds than for drivers who are 18 to 19 years old. Some car crashes are deadly.

Know the Facts!

The crash risk of teen drivers without adult supervision is increased with each teen **passenger** in the car.

People say that raising the driving age will keep beginning drivers and others safer from car crashes.

Tougher
TESTS

Some people want to keep the minimum driving age the same. They say that the problem isn't age. Instead, they believe people should be judged by their abilities. They think that teens should have tougher tests to pass before earning their driver's license.

Many driving tests only look at basic skills. Harder tests would ensure that young drivers have the skills needed for real-world situations. Teen drivers could also be required to have a certain number of practice hours or be required to have their learner's permit or restricted license for longer.

Know the Facts!

A study from Utah showed that Washington, Massachusetts, and Maryland had the hardest driving tests in the United States.

Driving tests usually look at basic skills such as turning, changing lanes, and parking.

Maturity
MATTERS

Some people say that teens aren't mature enough to drive. Driving gives someone the power to get from place to place, but it also comes with a risk. Cars are heavy machines that can hurt and even kill people.

People argue that teens as young as 16 don't have the same ability to control their feelings and actions as an adult does. This can affect, or play a part in, their driving. Scientists say that a person's brain isn't fully mature until about the age of 25. That's why some believe the higher the minimum driving age, the better.

Know the Facts!

According to the CDC, drivers aged 15 to 19 in deadly car crashes were more likely than any other age group to be **distracted**.

The CDC says that teens are more likely than adults to make decisions that can lead to serious car crashes.

Learning by
DOING

Some people say that teens should learn to drive at a young age because they can only learn by doing. The younger a teen is able to get a permit or license, the more time they'll have to practice driving with a parent or other adult.

These people say that if the minimum driving age is raised to 18 or 19, then young people will have less time to practice driving. They might be in college or working at a job. It's often easier for college students and people with jobs to have their own car, so it can be good for teens to learn to drive in high school.

Know the Facts!

The CDC says crash risks are high during the first months after getting a license. Some people argue this is because of inexperience and not age.

Driving takes skill, and the way to learn a skill is through many hours of practice.

Get a
MOVE ON!

Driving is just one form of **transportation**. Teens can also walk or ride their bicycle if they aren't going too far. These and other forms of transportation get teens moving. Some people say that teens should get as much exercise as possible, especially since they sit so much in school. If they aren't able to drive cars because the driving age is raised, they might choose forms of transportation that also act as exercise.

Other forms of transportation also harm the **environment** less than driving. Cars and trucks can increase **global warming**, while walking and biking do not.

Know the Facts!

A 2018 Gallup poll showed that 70 percent of younger Americans (aged 18 to 34) were worried about global warming.

It might be healthier for people and the planet if there were fewer drivers.

Busy
LIVES

Many people argue that teens need cars to keep up with their busy lives. Many teens want to have a job to make extra money or save for college. Teens also take part in sports and other **extracurricular** activities.

Raising the driving age would mean that many 16-year-olds and 17-year-olds wouldn't be able to work unless their job was close to home. They might also miss out on being able to do an after-school activity if an adult couldn't drive them there or pick them up. Letting 16-year-olds and 17-year-olds drive can help adults too.

Know the Facts!

In 2021, 54.4 percent of people aged 16 to 24 had a job.

Allowing teens to drive can open up new job opportunities so they can make money.

Who Should
DRIVE?

Some people are nervous about young drivers on the road. They think that young drivers are more likely to do risky things, like racing their cars or texting while driving. Other people say that driving at younger ages can give people more practice. They can learn from their parents or guardians while they're still living at home.

What do you think about these arguments? It's always important to look at both sides. You can use your experience as well as the facts to form your opinion!

Know the Facts!

The CDC says that teens and young adults have the lowest seat belt use of all age groups.

Should the driving age be raised?

YES

- Younger drivers are at a higher risk for car crashes.
- Younger drivers aren't mature enough to drive.
- Teens could be spending more time walking or biking instead of driving.
- Young drivers may do risky things like racing and texting while driving.

NO

- Age isn't as important as ability, so driving tests should be made harder.
- Teens need time to practice driving and gain experience.
- Teens will be limited in the activities and jobs they can do without a license.
- Adults can teach young drivers important driving skills while they're still living at home.

Being able to drive is important to many teens.

GLOSSARY

distract: To draw a person's thoughts or attention to something else.

environment: The natural world around us.

extracurricular: Describing an activity that's not part of a regular school day.

global warming: The warming of the earth's atmosphere as a result of the human use of fossil fuels.

license: An official paper giving someone the right to do something.

mature: Relating to the condition of being fully grown or developed, like an adult.

minimum: The lowest possible number allowed.

passenger: Someone who rides on a plane, car, or bus.

permit: A printed document from a government or organization that allows someone to own or do something restricted.

risk: The possibility that something bad will happen.

supervision: The act of watching and directing what someone does or how something is done.

transportation: The act of moving people or things from one place to another.

For More
INFORMATION

WEBSITES

Staying Safe in the Car and on the Bus
kidshealth.org/content/kidshealth/us/en/kids/articles/car-safety.html#catout
Learning safety rules for riding in a car can be great practice for learning how to drive when you're old enough.

U.S. Rules of the Road
driving-tests.org/beginner-drivers/rules-of-the-road/
Review this website with a parent or guardian to get familiar with the rules of the road and how they keep people safe.

BOOKS

Decker, William. *Safe in the Car.* New York, NY: PowerKids Press, 2017.

Shea, Therese. *All About Bicycles.* New York, NY: Britannica Educational Publishing, 2017.

Taylor, Charlotte. *Highways and Roads.* New York, NY: Enslow Publishing, 2020.

Publisher's note to educators and parents: Our editors have carefully reviewed these websites to ensure that they are suitable for students. Many websites change frequently, however, and we cannot guarantee that a site's future contents will continue to meet our high standards of quality and educational value. Be advised that students should be closely supervised whenever they access the Internet.

INDEX

A

activities, 18, 21
adult, 4, 8, 12, 13, 14, 20

B

bicycles, 16, 21
brains, 12

C

car crashes, 8, 9, 12, 13, 14, 21
cars, 4, 8, 12, 16, 18, 20
countries, 6

D

distracted drivers, 12
driving test, 6, 10, 11, 21

E

environment, 16, 17
exercise, 16
experience, 14, 20, 21

G

global warming, 16

J

jobs, 14, 18, 19, 21

L

learner's permit, 4, 6, 10, 14

M

maturity, 4, 12
minimum driving age, 4, 5, 6, 8, 10, 12, 14

O

opinions, 20

P

parents, 14, 18, 20, 21
passengers, 8
practice, 10, 14, 15, 20

R

restricted license, 6, 7, 10

S

seat belts, 20
sports, 18
states, 4, 5, 6
supervision, 4, 8, 14